MY PIECE OF THE PUZZLE

MY PIECE OF THE PUZZLE

Doren Robbins

A Lynx House Book
Eastern Washington University Press

Cover art: Chaim Soutine (1894–1943), *Le petit pâtissier* (The little pastry cook), oil on canvas, c. 1922. 60¼ x 26 inches (153 x 66 cm). Courtesy of the Portland Art Museum, Portland, Oregon. Ella M. Hirsch Fund Purchase.

Cover and interior design by Christine Holbert

Library of Congress Cataloging-in-Publication Data

Robbins, Doren.
 My piece of the puzzle / Doren Robbins.
   p. cm.
 "A Lynx House book."
 ISBN-13: 978-1-59766-038-9 (alk. paper)
 I. Title.
 PS3568.O229M9 2008
 811'.54—dc22

                    2007050549

Eastern Washington University Press
Spokane and Cheney, Washington

 CONTENTS

Part One

Part Two

PART ONE

FOUR FAMILY

We didn't know anything—we were four people
living in a one-bedroom fourplex and they couldn't pay

the Seaboard Finance Company again. We didn't know
what was what. My oldest aunt,

the communist with a purple-silver perm, showed us
a woodblock print and a drawing of Käthe Kollwitz's mothers

and children—the wall the mothers made around their bodies—
we didn't really get it. My own mother's expressions bewildered me.

I remember my father washing the dishes and my mother sitting
at the cutting board drying them, crying and talking about Seaboard,

"Ralph, how the hell are we going to pay Seaboard next month?"
The dish towel in front of her eyes bunched into fetal curves.

Packets of art reproductions came in the mail. Where did they get money
for that? She kept them in a drawer in the kitchen for my brother. Gauguin,

Van Gogh, Rembrandt, Michelangelo, Toulouse-Lautrec. Rembrandt
drowned my eyes with that portrait of himself, of the bottom of his eyes,

at the end. My brother tried to copy it, he was always drawing.
Ma said she could just give him her eyebrow pencil wherever she took

him and he would sit there on the floor and draw people's faces
and women's legs. My brother knew more. When she broke down

he took me out of the kitchen, he covered me, I always had reason
to trust him. He saw more misery than I did. My mother and her

3

three brothers raised him during the war and for a few years after.
The faces in the Kollwitz drawing and woodblock print scared me —

where were the fathers? Familiar mother's big hands
leather covering children.

It was the early fifties. The dieseled ashes of Germany and more than
Germany were still a fresh part of the soot in the eucalyptus in our yard.

She feared that the eucalyptus would fall on our bedroom and kill us in our
sleep. She had it cut down. We didn't say a thing. We were four people

living in a one-bedroom fourplex. Years after that — at the old La Brea
Theater — the four of us cried out of our eucalyptus mouths.

We were watching the film *The Heart Is a Lonely Hunter*. We didn't know
the book. I read it all in two days when I got it. Kollwitz's mothers showed

on the ash mouths and eyelids of those two mute guys in the book, they
struggled to watch over each other.

I follow it that way in my mind. I can't separately reason that I'm here
feeling this and not back in the Longwood Avenue kitchen

or in the La Brea movie theater lobby with what I felt.
Experience has not nearly increased accuracy enough.

Working with my father in the garage I used to make
boats out of scrap wood and metal. My connection

to assembling things, my connection to accuracy
began there. But I didn't know anything. Some nails

and the hammer, some glue, some blowtorch
did it. We owe a lot to the materials. Every tool lives

in a shrine, every shrine stands in for
the other—it all gets mixed up: the mute lovers

with the ones at the sink, brothers reborn in a mother's towel
with the fragile wall of mothers, with the reborn

eucalyptus, with the ash mouths and eyelids,
with the sheet-metal sail.

WHAT RETURNS

At Pico and Normandy,
at the Greek festival,
I was thinking in Greek

about my brother
sending a postcard from the
archeological museum in Athens—

a color photo of a bronze, a boy jockey,
about my age, fourteen,
in midair, riding alone.

I pinned the rider
by the night lamp, mounted
on the invisible horse,

a 4" x 6" card, his legs clasping
the body not there, still carrying him,
the light gold-brown in the lamp shade.

And the Greeks placed him, still
admiring him, suspending him
high up over the wood base,

the delight of the boy uplifted,
astride, held up by a steel bar,
his boy's face carried

straight ahead, fast,
and without his horse,
for now an imagined horse.

At the Pico and Normandy of Greece,
on my journey, in the almost bare
corridor, in the roped-off exhibition,

the boy jockey rode his racehorse,
pounding ahead, rediscovered,
the Aegean Sea somewhere,

retrieved for him, reassembled —
twelve years after my brother —
the horse, the blue-green bronze;

the divers raised the pieces up,
what care, drawn to the place,
drawn by their tentative maps,

the approximate knowledge,
forelegs and hind legs
striding, the neck fur blown

toward his hand again, the force,
the shape of the leg muscles
stretched as though struggling up

through layers of the sea floor,
through all the outlasted currents,
to him, really, to anyone

standing by that frail rope
missing the lost animal,
returned to the land,

to the imagined racetrack,
to the brothers Pico
and Normandy,

to a brother
missing a brother.

AGAINST ANGELS

Somebody asked me,
but I'm not going
to argue about

the topic of the soul,
deduce or repeat
inductive facts

for its evidence.

For me it's what
the Alsatian poet meant
when he wrote of

the "precision of
the indefinable."

And I've risen
in the plain rinse
of that precision

a couple times before,
and before that.

But I don't have any
depth for angels,
not Lawrence's angel

which he thought was
made when a man's soul
blended into

a woman's soul. And not
Rilke's angels—their beauty—
which he believed

was nothing but
the beginning
of a terror

he could just
barely endure.
I think there is

something somewhat
neurotic about
the prestige

and rarity
of angels—so,
I'll stay plain,

even crude,
a turkey buzzard
among herons

and ruby-crowned kinglets.
And I would be cautious
of angels—Constantine the Great,

for instance, contracted leprosy
after dreaming of an angel
pouring water on him.

BUKOWSKI IN LOVE

Really, Bukowski had it pretty good
living ecstatically and bitterly, living drunken
and sexual, and finally eating better than Li Po
or John Clare, eating regular at The Sizzler
in spite of the 123.2 pollution plagues
and 419 ongoing wars, in spite of his
own acne-ugliness. Sitting in cracker crumbs,
pork 'n' bean stains on the T-shirt with his
own face lithograph-reproduced on the front
and the back—recorded catastrophic alcohol
illumination coma bleeding gut, casual desperate
whore friendships in rundown flats, really
sickened self-hate lucidity struggle
fury against his demented ass-pounding father.
Recorded bestial labor in slaughterhouses, DTs
in flophouses—mostly a clear read of
the consequences for some of the selves
including himself, in the world,
legally, illegitimately cheated,
until he finally got lucky:
the best include the worst. The Linda
he dedicated his work to in the end must've
endured a lot. Old Jew in-law musician
uncle, talking a month before he died
about his first love in Warsaw, said to me,
"Because of her, I learned to play the violin."

DVAYDA

Always the precise way she put things together, sewed things
together, delight singing in Yiddish and Russian doing it, her wrist pains
doing it—delighting in theirs.

And always her offering more, which was her direct madness—sometimes
endearing, sometimes irritating: her "more." Made patches and sewed
more patches more; cooked for you, refused to let you help more, refused

to let you refuse more, loved you more than you wanted, more than you
asked, more than you feared.

And what a dramatic lover she must've been, whether she meant it or not.
What a liquefying opera she must've surged and spilled over if it was
anything like her singing, and her filling bowls and piling bowls with fruit.

I alternated being welcoming and turning my back to her.
I was never easy, at ease, never the kind of spongy matter I needed to be
to endure or con someone so I might thrive on that attention pouring and

pouring. Maybe some lack. Maybe a panel missing someplace in me.
But I don't give a damn, I'm not the available vacuum, there's a floor
underneath what I contain and receive. What a floor.

And even as I say it, even as I'm backing away from her again, I'm kissing
the lids and brows of my great aunt's eyes, I'm floored by her "more"
whatever she meant by it, whomever she really sought to fill with it,

or empty herself from, keeping her pot roasts and honey cakes flying out
of the oven, her kugels flying sweet enough,
or a little more, "A *bisel* more?"

piled on the table steaming for you, more?
"*Ziskeyt* sweetness," more? And leaving the table
with her watering can in the middle of serving,

in the middle of eating, feeding and also singing to her plants,
watering and dusting them and showing how she used to
cut scraps for her two dogs

dead all these years, mimicking the way she pleaded to each
and how they yelped for the brisket dangling from her mouth,
and giving a little more to the smaller, smarter one who

came down from her lap and waited quiet under the table.
Even while she talked about the two dogs, she mixed up nephews
with philodendrons, sisters-in-law's diseases with the purest garlic
and fish broth, mixed up longing and praise for her husband with imported

holiday plates, still talking about her dogs. She wasn't just
talking about dogs, it was always her ritual, her overflowing,
she was talking about her code of more, even in her endearments

praising dogs, it seeped through, the likeness of something else
connecting one ritual of more with another, more than dogs and tailoring,
more than carefully trimmed meat scraps, more than

getting on a downtown bus to find the strongest buttons because you
wouldn't know where to look. More than setting aside more for her
favorite niece, and a little more for the one who hated the favorite.

SOME TRAVELING MUSIC

For all I knew, the Fats Domino of the accordion
was going back to Athens. He smelled of oregano and sweat,

and he woke me with his music and the sour flow of Turkish smoke.
He wasn't dressed any better than the one in the news they called

a looter, who lives in a box on Spring Street in L.A.
I was listening to the basouki of the Sonny Boy Williamson

of the Greek slum in Istanbul–and I thought the Etta James
of the rattraps of Ankara took everything out of me—

I slept on the deck for the fifth time in five overnight voyages,
laid within the moisture that muted the burning

in my throat. And it was almost ceremonious the way they seated
the Stéphane Grappelli of the blind, and how with gratitude

they watched his hands adjust the strings.
They were half an hour into their music

when the mandolin player stopped to finish off his brandy
and the basouki player waved for him not to stop playing

with a gesture signaling it was a disgrace to Stéphane Grappelli,
and the Little Anthony of the mandolin lit two cigarettes

and hurriedly placed one between Sonny Boy Williamson's lips
who then tilted and closed his eyes again. If it weren't for

their driven music, if it weren't for the village—I'm not sure exactly
which village—it was in the mountains of Crete—there was

nowhere to pay for a place to sleep and no one offered—
I took my pack into a field—I'm saying there are such remote villages,

so many ruined paths, unpredictable depths, and I stood there
adding up my arms—my dealing arm, my sawing arm, my arm

that squawks pressing out marks of blue ink, and the tight arm,
the pleading arm, the arm that binds me, the arm I see through,

the arm unarmed, and the arm that will return to
the weeds and the microorganisms with their rows of

patient teeth. I lay there waiting it out, cataloguing my
arms, adding up the stalks of which I am the fruit—I'm saying

there are such remote villages and the Lady Day
of the Greek Netherlands has not sung of them yet.

I won't sing of them either—the Odysseus of false starts,
the one who goes on composing his ode to a sponge.

And I will have left Heraklion

with the Little Esther Phillips of Marseilles,
with her hands that were roughed up from working

in a Michelin tire factory—with her hands that waved through
cigarette smoke to the music of the Fats Domino of the accordion

playing to the crew in the boiler room. With her cracked hands
she was waving as we stopped on the narrow spiral stairway

leading back down to the lower deck
where the curve in the bend of the stairs was not

wide enough for the two of us, and Little Esther turned
so the movement of the melody in her hands continued

over the railing. And I will have left Switzerland

after having seen The Cellophane Girl
do her strip, I will have left the Roman Carnival after

hearing Snake the Talking Head speak, and
I will have left genuinely uncertain of what they did

with the rest of his body, I will have left
not understanding how a woman could be

pressed into such a thimble of cellophane.
And I will have passed through Greece

after completing my ode to sloth,
written on a food wrapper after getting poisoned on Corfu.

I will have finished it after drinking mountain tea
in the greasy heat of a *kafenion* after two days and nights

of sweating and shitting. I will have written it down
with my arm that wasn't poisoned. And it will have

come to me after the dream of a drowned pelican
eating from my plate, it will have been revised only once,

sitting at the kitchen table, while I was trying to make out
the barren layers from the sprouting layers

of the dusk sanding my window.

HOWARD MUELLER'S FATHER

When I talk about Mueller's father I'm talking about a closed-up man,
a man all knuckles and eyes, "a bodyguard,"

my older brother said, for someone big in Vegas.
I'm talking about the fear of answering him incorrectly

when we would see him in the mornings at Canter's Deli—
a giant at the counter always

in that navy blue suit, asking why Howard wasn't with us
or was Howard's girlfriend okay? We were fifteen, and we nodded

and bullshitted him never saying a thing about Howard's "girlfriend"
whom he socked—once we were sure of—and forced

drunk one night, and that too we kept quiet about.

I'm talking about the dread of looking at his eyes—that he might

detect and resent the fear I had of him because I heard one night
he was stoned, and Howard's mood bugged him, and Howard
got smacked for it, and blood sprayed over the stove. And

some of us who had fathers or stepfathers nodded like we knew it
in our own way when it was told. When I talk about

Mueller's father I'm talking about that Buick Electra, midnight blue,
with a Cadillac engine, a "gift" from the bosses in Reno—

I'm talking about his wife who never came out
when we were over and who used to be
"a chorus line beauty,"

I'm talking about the apartment they lived in
where Howard slept on a cot, and that

it was "temporary."

When I talk about Mueller's father I'm talking about the fork
that always looked stubbed in his hand, and about his eyes—
those little scourged crusts of ink. I'm talking about the fist

of a man that could take a fifteen-year-old boy to the kitchen floor—
cut him right at the entrance to himself entering

or answering back
against his will.

Nine years out of that neighborhood and I saw Mueller's father
in a shabby place I stayed in overnight between cities:

two rows of three mattresses lined together
over the spills and burns of a concrete floor

in a room about 20' x 20'
yet he was the real filth.

But I have to come down too much to depict him or I'm bitter
he returned and could be where I had to sleep,

or that I reentered his world,

or never left. And I watched him, not saying anything,

unrecognized by him as he went about with his function
to rent mattresses and to offer no paper in his toilet.

THE KINGS OF ALSEA

Held back two hours in Alsea and I went down
behind The Black Log Tavern toward the river,

its chlorinated back going toward the Black Log Woods.
Punishment was king or king enough.

Down there a pack of boys chased after a cat, the smallest one
yelling, "I got some rope, I got some rope!"

It was like I wasn't there at all when I called them over—
and when I came behind the tavern where I heard their voices

they were already down in fir woods yelling, kings, or each one
of them king enough—
                            came back around the Black Log

and went in through the back of the bar where the river swept under,
and one of the kings of Alsea pointed me out when
I came in. He wanted me to come push his wheelchair up to
the bar for him, and I said, "Okay, let's go." And he wanted me

to talk about the ficus tree with its leaves dropped off while the one
by the door was covered with tight buds—and I explained about
tree viruses and diseases. Then he ordered the guy next to me

to tie his broken bootlaces, and a woman walking in
from a cannery on the coast of mud

to come clean out bread stuck in his teeth and to button
his pants. And they did it while I held his fat hand

with all the spots, and he sang

about the fox that tore open a pumpkin to get at a mouse
that ate its way inside. Then he slurred something

about a knife that stood up on a plate when he entered
Warsaw—some other melody about burning cages

and the unstitched ground—as he trailed off about it saying
he was a petty man—maybe a king—or not much of king—
                                        but king enough
and that he's not the one to be pushed from place to place
but I will do, or the guy on the other side of him will do—

while he bitched about the lack of whiskey, the one tread left
on his right front tire, and every miserable puke he worked for.

I looked into his gray mouse eyes still open,
the chin slipped through cheap Scotch
to the shoulder. Through the unbuttoned shirt
I looked into the soldier's scar running
down to his hip and the tattoo
commemorating a battle in Pukchon—

"Fifteen years limping and struggling not to limp around
and that's the least of it, look at this," he was opening
his shirt, "Look at these marks, look at this dog, here, I could
never lift it away, it went dead on its paws, right here," he said,
pointing where the skin sagged with a gash.

And he was not the one and "the dog" was not the one
I wanted to notice me at all, but I too

have seen the knife standing on a plate, I saw the red stitch marks
that kept his nipple tied to the rest of the skin,

and I saw the struggle with "the dog" and I felt bound to it

and to what was happening there.

GOLDWATER DIED LAST WEEK

Goldwater died last week, finally. Several years of cancer, and heart this, and heart that. Not much to go on there.

Continuous dominant-culture sentimentalization on the news about his death. But we egged his presidential headquarters on Sunset Strip in '64, because our parents said he didn't give a shit about working people or minority people or immigrant people. Like who was left? But I don't know what we were really thinking. I know what I think now. Maybe some of us were better informed in '64.

I've been back on the coast for several weeks. Out there, the kelp beds remain sleepless, some kind of circulatory feeding and dying trough. They give me anxiety. I tried to idealize that world, but I've been back long enough and worked at enough shit jobs to stop idealizing anything that happens on the coast.

Returned here after the virus I had for eleven months—whatever it was— you couldn't do a thing. Someone recommended a high colonic. I wasn't too sure about that. And what if during such a procedure the doctor is naked? I felt like I was chewing down to the particles of a mirror to get through the low-down virus, and even that image might just as well be another inflation to cushion myself. And problems like these used to strike me with less force. Or is it kindness to remember it to myself that way?

However that may be, as a result: seven weeks I went off everything, everything! Wine and caffeine, kishka and cognac, Lame Deer and Black Elk, pork-tits and chili fries. When it all passed, I was well enough to go out again and chip away with my finishing hammer at the ice caked on the gate hinges out back. Farther up north I had the same habit, or was it necessity to deal with how such weather transforms things? Habit. Discipline. Both. More. No kelp visible farther north, only ice. I smoked a brittle cigar, my mind was brittle.

Now I remember, *now I remember*, I couldn't do anything any longer with my hammer up there. It was the night after I dreamed of myself with two backsides. In the same dream I had two sets of teeth. I was eating a dog's head in the dream, then the flies ate through my collar and buttons, flies ate my hair and nails, they ate the shoes I just bought, a fact so annoying and perilous to me—even after waking up from the dream, I couldn't bear it. God damn those flies!

PART TWO

DIGNITY IN NAPLES AND NORTH HOLLYWOOD

I walked around Naples detached, my washing soap wrapped
in a map of Florence. Smoking constantly, I stopped
to roll up another as one burned out. Then crossing an alley

a child wrapped in torn things startled me—
he was beating a small cat with a plastic bag
of garbage—I stopped him by his arm

and a young woman dashed out of her flat
and rapped him hard on the side of his face
reprimanding him in the kind of tone that said

she'd caught him doing it before—then she cursed me
for handling her boy so roughly. I went down another street
filled with ragged people in dark glasses, heavy rogues

in tight pants, the sunken-chested, the cross-eyed and the stoned,
losing her and her sadistic boy. I kept moving.
I came up to a tilted corner of stained curbs, of black market

Marlboros sold for a dime, a corner of broken-down carts,
opera blaring over geranium boxes, dirt busting the joinery
of the boards, I was at the corner of dirty swallows

and dumped ashes, hinges pulling away from doors and shutters,
fleas, pregnant women with no shoes. I gave my bag of dates
to a beggar and he bowed, inventing the corner of dignity

in the most crushed layer of Naples, and I bowed back
handing him tobacco with my maimed indifference, my sweating
frailties, and my mind that would go on insisting my journey here

was my odyssey, my homecoming, since it was always a matter
of finding out who was maimed, who was bumbling, frail, insisting—
to find out who, to turn against the numb crust

I surrounded myself with, resistant in the most crushed layer—
to see who it was with little regret, with little rejoicing—
to find out who and proceed, or fail to find out

and proceed—because my myth was to go on feeding
the butcher with nine arms I would finally tear myself open with.
My odyssey, my return, was not to Naples, after all,

or to Chania or Rhythimnon, but to North Hollywood, where I lost it
screwed over from too much wine—except for a few bucks
I lost the whole check gambling in North Hollywood where I lasted

less than two hours. And a guy I knew who was making it at that table
said he would loan me $25 for groceries if I would stop.
The wine wearing off—driving back—peeling down that road

to some other layer, needing to enter it one way or another—
speeding down the hill where Sepulveda Boulevard swings
below the freeway overpass

—racing to the lamenting sax of Coleman Hawkins—
ready enough to take the sharp curve at the bottom, jerking rhythmically
to the music I kept turning up.

LATINA WORKER

Then I notice through a triple-Americano-awakening moment,
in the mall food court, a young Latina cleaning around by the chrome rail
at Sbarro Pizza. Maybe a Guatemalan, possibly Salvadoran or
Honduran—

could've been Argentinean or Columbian, Chilean, Bolivian,
Panamanian—good chance a Peruvian, Venezuelan, Nicaraguan, Mayan,
Toltec, Sephardic, Huichol coffee plantation or U.S. Fruit Company

or tobacco company or auto industry slave labor robot or CIA-trained
death squad Guardia Nacional butchery massacre survivor.

Several tables down from mine—roughly stacking chairs on tops
of tables—cussing in Spanish, in the mall food court, she hates her job,
I hate her job.

WITH THE LITTLE ESTHER PHILLIPS
OF MARSEILLES

The singer Katrina Solonge, muse of three poems,
Little Esther Phillips of Marseilles, gave me her drawings

of helicopter pilots dumping
murdered Greek students

onto a remote island in the Cyclades
—night of the military takeover in Greece—

the pilots bestial and robotic
in their headphone gear.

She gave them to me inside that room
with a seven-foot door in Chania

where everything ended, a room rented
from a guy who smoked rapidly and choked out

words like his balls were in his stomach and stared
at Katrina's ass when he wasn't staring

at her tits, when he wasn't looking at her hair
like he wanted to chew on it. He rented

his little hole of a room for too much, way
too much, and he was in a place remote enough

that he could be impassive about it.
And his eyes moved erratically, stimulating

some dread, but it wasn't fear of him I felt.
Inside the room in Chania things were

coming apart. I was one of the helicopter pilots,
the cord to my headphones was broken,

but the broken cord wasn't some
broken-cock symbolism, it was the same thing

that broke nineteen years later with Sara Karakos.
There I was, talking with Isaac Babel

about what it's like trying to kiss your own ear.
I was looking right at Sarah K. beside the hibachi grill,

which was too small, and some of the bars
weighed down with ground meat

had broken and caved in on the coals.
Someone stepped from behind Isaac Babel

and brought her tongue through her
lips down to my hand

when she kissed it. I was a little stunned.
If I was supposed to know what I risked

by leaving my hand under her mouth, I didn't
know it yet. There I am in the dream

splicing and tightly wrapping
the wires back into the cord. And I look good

in that helicopter pilot getup, right down
to the mute expression

I fit into it.

AT THE DOOR WITH DEBUSSY

I'm standing by the door waiting for my ride, listening to Debussy
with the volume turned down, so I won't miss the horn.

All over again I remember the Sicilian stewards on the ship from Corfu
stowing plastic bags of garbage to sell in the port at Sardinia — the waves

resting indigo-tinted again in my mind, the mothers and old crones
wrapped in black shawls battling for bags of our garbage . . .

I'm recounting every stringent measure of vinegar, virgin olive oil, black
pepper and oregano — everything Fresselman wants me to remember for

the salad dressing, while he starts recounting his thirty-six-hour shifts
on Dexedrine as an air controller during the bombing of Cambodia.

And I'm watching his bony hand with the tattoo of a syringe grip and pour
the vinegar, measuring it as he walks, as I cut

two ten-gallon barrels of mushrooms with speed and grace
in under an hour, as expected.

Really it was something more like my apparition or my double standing
at the door, needing again some voyage — the ship from Corfu to Piraeus,

from Piraeus to Heraklion — always the possibility for some other life
I can enter once I turn this one down. I stood looking out the French door

waiting for a black Ford, smoking Wednesday's first cigarette, listening
to *Syrinx* by Debussy, wondering what wrong turn Debussy had taken

that he ended up lost or foolish enough and connected enough to the same
theme, while I waited there for my ride. What had the great Debussy

driven into, that the drama of a compulsive failed seduction in an old myth
would interest him beyond the fact that a woman was driven

to transform herself into something nonhuman to escape
the sweating animal cocksmith. I stood at the door trying to figure out

the most believable way to borrow against my check, because the owners
held back the first week's pay. I was there with Debussy playing randomly

from the classical station—a childless man not yet twenty-nine,
thinking through that myth about a kind of pleasure, the cruel

unchangeable transformation, the possibilities for more of the same,
and Fresselman's voice in my mind, Fresselman speaking yesterday

from the scar on either side of his forearm, amazed the bullet missed
the bone, going over a vegetable order, turning his arm this way and

the other, over and back, while he spoke.

BEFORE AND AFTER TAMPICO

to Raphael Escamilla

I always thought if it came down to it I would take off again,
go to the seaport of Tampico and continue that life
of drifting around, working my way as a cook

on a freighter to the Far East. I thought I could just
turn away from the straw through which everything bland
and everything functional swallowed

my forgettable name. I would stand in Tampico ready to leave
the Gulf of Mexico, the surf dark as burnt fat—and the whores,
absurd in their clothes that don't fit them, coming on to me

at the dock. And I would drink and eat with them while feeding
the skinny dogs prowling around the tables for scraps. And I would
admire those dogs because of their persistence, their sharp teeth, their

dexterous paws with unclipped nails. And maybe I would see
Raphael Escamilla in Tampico, that Indian face of his
more feminine than Vallejo's which was itself neither

male nor female—that face uncomplainingly driven along some
high wire without a net. I would like to have seen again
Raphael Escamilla with that Indian face the clerk looked at impatiently

while he counted from a roll of singles and fives
that would get his last two sisters smuggled into Mexico.

Out there in Tampico, where my life would
change, I would like to see Raphael who first put the idea of
cooking on a ship in my mind, who therefore put Tampico in my mind.

Escamilla, whom I was always paired with, working weekends, overtime,
hustling the waitresses, pointing, hinting, and leering at what hung
to the middle of his leg. He said he would've worked his way to Indonesia

if he had to, cooking on a ship, to escape what was happening
in Morazán, to escape *los diablos*, to escape the university of
the Green Beret, and Immigration. I would like to have seen Raphael

Escamilla again in that moment when he was sending the money back
and he was confident—how could a man not be confident
who hid in a pile of corpses when the National Guard came busting

and poking with rifle butts cracking two of his ribs, and he lay still
not making a sound? I would like to be there watching him count
the money for his two sisters. I would kiss his face, awkwardly

the way males in my family kiss their brothers or fathers, I would kiss
him having thought I would never see him again, glad neither of us
had to end in L.A. for good—as long as it wasn't Morazán or at

the Río Sumpul, but in the seaport of Tampico with our cook's knives
each wrapped deep in a towel—standing at the dock with the whores
in their tight audacious clothes, and the skinny dogs I admire for

their mindless tenacity, and with Escamilla as I always see him, confident
with that roll of singles and fives, confident as though what he sensed
was coming might not come—even though, I remind him again,

what's coming isn't going to take the least hesitant step
off its course.

DON'T FEED THE SIGN

After the rain stopped,
I went out to the palisade
for a walk and to feed
roasted peanuts to the squirrels.
A new sign up there warned me
not to feed them or other "vermin."
But I'm not someone going to
get rabies from a squirrel.
Screw the sign. I prefer
squirrels to the upholders
of these signs especially,
and to the painters of
the signs, though,
with a couple of exceptions
I suspect for
the painters it was
just a job. I always feed
squirrels and birds
that aren't so picky about
what I've got. I used to
feed them with my wheezing
emphysemic grandfather who
usually walked around the park
with a pigeon on his hat.
And I feed them now with
my three-year-old nephew
so he will learn the trick of
reaching them and feeding them
from own his hand, so as to find out
what they are like, and know
his distance, and know
their swift movement.

It's a little thing, their endless
appetite, their elegance, what
a three-year-old remembers, my
optimism, the squirrels' filth,
their agile balance and grip,
their fur more lustrous
than human hair.

MY HAT UP NORTH

We were supposed to be considering
how much to offer on the house where
a family was renting, but you can

never look to me to move
renters out. No stomach
for that at all. Enough people already

want to think all kinds of
shitty things about me. The house
with peeling walls surrounded

on all sides by deciduous cedar trees
was the place where the realtor (when I told her
I was a carpenter) pointed out to me

that she knew the main contractor in town
and said she could put me in touch with him.
Then asked in a casual tone,

"You're a Christian, aren't you?"

That was during the time when all types
of people started wearing baseball caps.
But I don't think so many of them were

identifying with a team or
advertising some product or
even trying to keep the cancer sun

off their heads and faces—I think most
everybody in baseball caps was trying
to stay a little hidden or just trying

to keep the tops of their heads on, so to speak.

And it wasn't just a fad—even the realtor
wore a cap. Hers came from the college
in town and carried its mascot, a raging duck,

above the brim. Usually I wore a fishing hat
with nothing written on it. Back then
I even tried wearing a fez but

only once, because I looked like a clown
with my thick hair sticking out on the sides.
Sometimes I wore a Tijuana sombrero

with a bullfight stitched on the brim.
That was the one. Even with a broken thread
and a small hole where the bullfighter's cape let

the bull's horns brush the cloth,
it was my favorite hat.
My sombrero, it had part of a scene

stitched on felt unintentionally cut out,
so it was the illusion of violence
rather than what always happens, it was

just a man dancing with a beast.

ANOTHER SIDE OF PISGAH

I thought it was going to be one more day
of sopping up chemicals and dust in crawl spaces
or unventilated attics, not another side of Pisgah,

not another side of the stewing lily pads
in Vern Adkinson's water garden. And of all things
not an evening primrose partly burnt at mid stalk

that was going to open me up. One more day
of tar, I thought, and the fingers
the way they are stapled into the knuckles,

and the throat rising the way it does
out of its lapped collars of hair,
not the enclosed skin floating,

not those daubed lichen islands reopened,
not the permeable green pallor they rise out of
the live oak with, and not the clogged webs

in the pine trunk that would
draw me in. I sat by the dropped fins
and thorns of raspberries

watching a hawk moth and remembering
almost nothing about its entomology,
but watching the hawk moth with its greed

(that I relate to) and with its dissident daylight routine
(that I also admire), and the long tubular snout
draining everything from the fractured morning glory

and the poppy with its moistened bowl
of paper lips. And just as good
to be one of the red ants, I thought,

watching them rush out of their cone-brimmed
slit of dirt with white eggs in their mouths.
And just as good to be a red ant that doesn't return,

that makes it only long enough to save a white egg
under the stiff brushes of moss, the white pods,
the pine roots lapped with dying clover.

I didn't know what they were abandoning.
Then I had the premonition I'd pay
for not knowing. But maybe I wouldn't,

I thought. Maybe I paid enough already.
Maybe it was just one more day as a carpenter
as it had once been just one more day

as a line cook, or a paper grader, or a health spa
clean-up crew backup man. One more day of
no accounts, no car, or doubling the play-off series bet

to hopefully get the car out of the shop.
One more day when I entered the rectangle
that had no corners and not the door

of a drywall contractor or the office
of the manager-cop of a bar and grill where
I was consigned as a broilerman for three years—

so that while I was in there,
so that while that geometry suddenly existed,
another life no more or less improved

resumed without me—so that really
it was just another day when I forgot
how things were divided, another day

between the sheathings, another day
standing over the hole in the table
which corresponds in its way to the division,

another day getting used to the sewn-up feeling,
getting used to the watery lock I move within,
getting used to not envying or despising

the waterproof world either. Or it's not
another day of anything—
just some downward current

painting me with its hunger.
And I'm not going to bet
it won't dismantle me

again. I'm not going to bet a thing on it,
or that I'll get used to it,
that I'll get over it, or

that I could possibly answer
why I'm wasted and mended one way
and then another, why all the extremes,

and why I seclude myself in them.
I thought it was just another day of going down
to the Willamette River where it runs by Pisgah,

another day of going down to the Oasis Market
for my coffee and some oranges. But now—forget it,
now all of my past husks are speaking

from a napkin, and from the hole in the table,
and from a white egg waiting to be picked up.

PART THREE

MY PIECE OF THE PUZZLE

Studio City, 1979, my last cook's job,
one less time I can say now

I wasn't such a prisoner there
as I let people think, and one less time

I don't have to believe thinking
the opposite impression would matter,

I can just relax my ass and remember
how the wine from two nights before or two

decades before changed my flow,
and that I have one less Mr. Timi

looking over my shoulder while I
do prep work on the lettuce and fruit,

and one less Lubricci running us around
the kitchen because his giant friend

who built the tables and booths was
chasing one of the Beverly Hillbillies' grips

in the South Bay. One less time
I have to forget for one less minute

that I was stumbling after less
than one small piece of my puzzle —

and one less paranoid or self-righteous
or justifiable suspicion about those

that worked there and never acted puzzled.

No more trips to Studio City
working five nights a week to make it

in the pantry of a small
Continental restaurant. And how

was such a place even going to
break even, operating as it did

upstairs from a men's gymnasium?
One less junker I have to drive in

over the canyon to work, though
I was glad to have that old

Plymouth plain-clothes-cop-looking Belvedere
chrome clicking under my work shoes.

One less weight lifter drinking some parsley,
beet and egg mixture on the deck below

where we sat on our break in peace.
One less balancing act getting the right pec

to meet up with the left. And one less day
handling the Cornish hen skeleton my mind

was getting deboned down to the equivalent of,
and one less talking styled hair and cashmere

and tasseled loafers Lubricci, who inherited
the whole thing after he failed

as a tenor in Bologna and got fed up
as a Jesuit monk in Milan,

and then found Frank "The Giant" in L.A.
One less session working on squeezing

a twenty-five-cent raise out of
Mr. Timi, his backer once

the inheritance started to dry up.
No more slow service in The Chinese Palace,

really some drinker's hole with
painted-over windows and the worst slop ever,

and I ate it all, sick of eating with Lubricci
or the waitresses or the other cooks, though

I was after Patricia, but there was Jody
who was herself fixated on Raoul

the busboy-musician, third cousin of
a shaman from Venezuela. One less field

of wild anise on one side where
the restaurant banked against the hill.

One less fight with Jody while I worked there
and we lived together five months. One less

pot of long rice smashed and spilled down
on the counter, one less guitar lesson

for her, which was really a lesson
in Venezuelan fucking. One less fake

Indian rug we kept under our mattress,
and one less Jody lifted and stroked

already moist through her hair
with the pleasure that is the most precious.

No more talks with Patricia, both of us
drunk in the car after the weekend shift,

hysterical afterwards about her brother
raping her for six years before she left

for an ashram in Florida where you hand over
your shoes and your dental records

and your money with your application.
One less Christmas card from her out of

San Rafael, Seattle, Tucson before
she disappeared into the Sea Organization

of Scientology. Remember Studio City,
the headlights glinting out of the curved road

down to the valley, one less time, coming over that canyon
with one less look that still didn't look right.

And one less vinegar jar leaking
over the sink—not another

missing handle on the freezer door
that came off during the day shift

and no one could find and I worked with it
missing. Not another night the oils and herbs

tan my apron, which was a sign of knowing
which oils and which herbs. One less Wednesday

smoking in the car before my night shift.
One less twilight with its layered diamond leaves.

AS MUCH AS YOU CAN

I'm eating over the complaining root alone.
This isn't a meditation on pleasure. Pleasure is always
divided into two: having it, and misery. That stays
the same. More where that came from. Something else
stamps desire with its form, something I haven't always
been cautious about, and I let myself think of
as a kind of puzzle or riddle to be acted out,
something that works through on its own, and I would
face it when it grew transparently sanded-through enough
to see. That's when I would look. But
it didn't happen quick enough. It doesn't always
stop soon enough. What I mean is: Not only my damage.
What I mean is: Sometimes you have to measure
a snake's ass while it's alive. That's the way I see it now.
The way I see it now—it's almost always 4:00 A.M.
And my eyes are starting to go more than a little.
Some of my teeth are going. The hope is:
nothing's next.

I'm eating over the pages of a book I brought back
from London, held open to a series of photos
of ancient bronze and marble sculptures of Greek gods.
Some have chipped heads and lips—in fact, the arms and cock
of Apollo, and the erotic feet and pelvis of Aphrodite
had been worn off, eaten away. The hope is:
from long use.

Halfway through my wine I get fixated
on a bronze sculpture of the sea goddess, Thetis,
riding a sea monster. And with the damned crumbs

all over, I stayed at the table looking at
the Greek woman, Thetis, riding
that sea monster, admiring
what appeared to me as her skill.

THAT OTHER AUNT

I hated to kiss that one aunt with her insane rooster-cackle when she laughed. Insanity enough for me. This aunt's husband was dead before he was thirty. She never remarried. She would physically force you tightly next to her while she inhaled most of the See's chocolate until one of the family saviors held her back, picked out the remains, and handed them around.

This aunt got my youngest uncle not only to fix things in her apartment but to drive her every place she needed to go. The good uncle: if there was green mold in his sour cream, if the bathroom light illuminated nothing but spiders, or his cat pissed in his only decent pair of shoes, he wouldn't have been moved from that one accommodating expression he showed to the world.

Thirty-five years that aunt was alone. I don't know what men and women did to her. I don't necessarily think now, after forty-five years of knowing men and women, that she would out-torment very many. She would certainly out-laugh any of them, but back then I thought she would contaminate me or I would end up desiring girls who would turn into mad cacklers like her— if I kissed her. So I hated all of them for pushing me at her face.

Was I supposed to be tender as a child? I don't know when that left if it was ever there, but if I had it, I didn't for everybody. I trust the child trying to hide behind the parent's leg. Everything threatened me, everything I didn't want, and that was my insanity and my sanity. I put a leg between revulsion and myself. And yet one of my cousins loved that aunt and scorned me and spilled soup on my hand for thinking her aunt was freaky.

Bending over to get a fallen spoon, I cut my palm on the way down on a machine screw I forgot in utter laziness and distraction to find a knob for and replace on a cupboard door. Cut skin layers below the surface, hard to protect those, enigmatic that it's hard. And it burns; it goes right along with what happens with obedience, what happens with resistance. I trip on the rug, I see her face.

THE EIGHTIES

But the eighties were different. One thing is clear about 1980
my daughter was conceived in ecstasy. Whatever her mother's

shape now and what's left of my own she'll know
what I mean when reading this, reading the hands, and reading

the eyelashes over the four depths, or reading the cuticles,
all the particles our particular heat made up—rushed up—

canopy of its own branches. In one particular 4" color matte-finish
Instamatic photo I'm thinking of, she'll look at it and know

with nothing or enough to make it seem like nothing
about the day nobody wanted and everybody still lives through

eight years later in the first installment. She'll see the current
her mother and I made. I know by her own magnetic stance

beside a young man, a bass player who works at Espresso Fire
where he gets ripped off like anyone in the restaurant business,

still, too desperate for money to give it up.
But that's too great a subject for my likes. I'm still

a little bit too much of a construction worker. That's what
the eighties were to me—demolition or construction. It was always

about materials or the lack of material or the immaterial.

Even though I sweated it out, even though I was
a carpenter-handyman longer than I wanted the eighties to last—

still, my daughter was conceived in ecstasy in 1980 when July's torch—
Venus—doesn't stop, and it was ecstasy in the early eighties just

to watch the small bitten fingers painting, spotted with paint, move
a wet brush around the crumbs, or just to hear her rhyming songs

to the red horse puppet. And her judgment-compassion picked up
from a children's book her grandparents could've written, a book

not published in America, it was about Buddha's life, she applied
some of it to my clumsiness—thanks for that I'm telling her now.

And from around the time she was two and a half—her fascination
with Venus. Always locating her in the twilit sky. And Venus

always enigmatic to me wild inexact flame

I lived out a way to tell her about.

I WENT THROUGH A BOX OF EMILY'S SHELL JEWELRY

I saw Emily all over again
when I went through the jewelry she made out of shells.
When I picked up a Frilled California Venus shell and a Milky Venus
        shell that lay together on a metal setting
without a clasp, a note beside them marked "next";

and when I picked up a fragmented letter with a dedication
to someone named Clair; and when I held a False Angel Wing shell
wrapped in linen cloth, held it
alone just to feel the weight
and smoothness of it in my hand—it was like
being there again with her
when we worked or made love after one of our walks. I could smell
her secretions in the room again, and I felt suddenly alert,
        missing her presence.

The illness she had spilled her
like so much spit. I didn't and still don't know what there is
to know about it. Even now, after eight years,
all of my theories, everything I name
becomes a synonym for some other complexity
or perplexity. Something took her over.

In the lane of dirt beside the garage wall, she planted her garden.
Her unwrapped cyclamen's pure purple or red cloth always opened
some libidinal gland riding my nerves. Her liquefying Dutch-broom
yellow and hot labial-colored alstroemeria's pink
did the same thing.
I never saw them before with someone
who could name them, plant and know them, and know
        how to care for them, without killing them. A pleasure to sit there,

my eyes holding it in. With her gone—all of those colors are faded
      in that part of me
            she made.

Everything exactly drilled, carefully fitted. Difficult to handle
such tiny screw anchors. And every anchor attached in strategically
crafted positions for the way the piece
should tilt, and hold.

I know little about the worth of her jewelry.
I mean, I don't know their fashion. Fashion always
made me sick. All fashion. I went through a box of jewelry
Emily made—mounted vaginal folds vital color inexact securely fixed
braided ornaments from the sea, from her hands.

NATURAL HISTORY

Tried to lift a swallowtail butterfly out of
a thick web, out of leg and wing fragments.
I think they were parts of moths and flies.
All the truncations, all the leaf chips,
dirty gauze strands, Chinese silver ash spores.
Held my thumb knuckle out for it to walk on.
That hesitating, that erotic clinging, that
flexing and trembling. At a garage window.
I forgot my tools inside the truck,
my work shoes by the pedals.
It came out on one thread. The window
behind the web was blank. Leather
insoles held the stained shapes of
my feet, those white swallows
pointing their beaks
at the underworld, pointing
at the carnivorous, pointing
and clinging. I was trying to lift it
through the leg and wing fragments
past the dry torso of a wasp.
Wrist bones secured with wire
in documentaries, fragmented in
my head. Mass grave photojournalism,
as usual quotas waiting for us,
incidental naturalism of our malice
documentaries went through my
interior gauze and webs. I was trying
to be steady. My hand close to the foot
below the wing, close to the breath
jumping on the rim of dirty strands.
To the antennae that looked moist,
to the remarkable fetal expression,
I held out my thumb knuckle.

CRAWDADDY

Watery shadows and grass ladders
at the bottom of that brook
where the crayfish
waited. And the girls
wanted him, they were
screaming for the animal
of white shields under
the water; they wanted
that crawdaddy, they
wanted to bring it back
to their aquarium, and they
emptied and gave me
a trashed cup they'd
been trying to catch
tadpoles in.
I thought a branch
the wind shook at
quick intervals signaled
someone else stepping
onto the path where
the brook converged,
but it was only
a swaying branch,
an illusory signal,
and I braced forward
on my elbows holding the cup;
and the crayfish waited, stopped
between rocks, then scuttled
sideways lifting its pincers
through lids of algae.
I pulled back the dense

layers with a stick,
touching the side
of it with a longer
branch. I didn't want
to catch that thing
at all. Pointed,
thick-armored, hellish
pincers raised, probably
why the seven- and eight-
year-old girls wanted
it and to touch
its face and
the curling antennae
with their own sticks.
They wanted the crawdaddy,
but I wasn't going to take it,
the back part of its body afloat,
rounded feminine-lipped tail
upturned, balanced to
propel the hardened
lopsided frontal
body and heavy
pincers forward, or
to the side.
They urged me
to scoop it into
the cup, but I
caught myself quick
enough and backed out.
There was some instinct
to see it clearly, to
take him in, to
recognize the odd
fit of the front
and the back,

the grotesque and
the delicate, neither
below the other. I stood
in the crawdaddy's water,
where he prepared to
battle more than our
sticks, if he had to. I stood
laced behind branches
praising something
about the foliage
and the dripping blossoms
the hummingbirds turned
and returned to
in May heat. Later,
I stood in the alley
of the apartment we
lived behind on 26th Street
off Arizona Avenue, stood
there shadowed by
the pepper tree branches
beside rubbish, alone,
next to thrown-out shoes
with wide heels ground down
to a drastic angle. I stood there
looking down at them empathizing abstractly
about the unknown life out of accord
that made them turn out that way.

THE RAINS

At a hotel off the Deschutes River, recorded in Bend, Oregon, the same
night going down for ice when I found a large moth inside from the rain.

Even dead it looked vibrant, resting on the inside corner
of a louvered windowsill.

Heavy layered fur neck, buffalo thick head. I saw all the way into the pearl
of running surf inside the moth's unshuttered eye, and the bloom in there
became clear a little piece of peel at a time.

Saw the loomed pieces stacked layers new petals lapped over a face within
the increased undergrowth, steadily withheld, unknown till then.

PART FOUR

PREDATORS' HOUR 2, OPEN ALL NIGHT

Not much on the bombing of Iraq twenty-four hours a day.
Not much on the bombing of military and fictional military
targets, and holiday photographs, religious icons
and peoples' bedrooms like ours—
and bullet factories, soccer balls, equipment
and hospitals, like ours—
the virgin son with a magazine
in the bathroom, the dictator's retreat,
and the playgrounds like ours,
and the men stacking eggplant crates,
the crates, the olive oil factory workers,
the metal cabinet factory workers,
the workers, infant strollers like ours,
plumbers' snakes, on fire . . .

And nothing I recall, nothing on Afghanistan, no reports
on the three-and-a-half million trying to escape to
one of the freezing borders during the bombing, they were
already starving before the attack began; they were already
imprisoned, disappeared, half burned to the ground from
the Russian invasion before, like ours . . .

Not a word: Iraqi civilian depleted uranium info bone smoked image dead.
No photojournalism clothes shredded burned in with skin, making one
skin, one melted mixed formed image, one pile of mouths burned shut.
I locked up looking at in my mind
after hearing a student now a vet tell it
through clenched teeth and weeping spit . . .

Not much on the eighty-seven journalists assassinated since the bombings began.
Not much on our own three-thousand-something dead, so far—thirty

thousand battle trauma cases, so far—eighteen-nineteen-year-old amputees
amputated from our sight . . .

And not much reported on immigrant Thai Vietnamese Philippine girls
doing it on the factory floor after work, a part of work, or strippers
dancing the shift right through their bleeding periods, or else—and who
figures that in?

Here and there remote articles on who's butchering the animals at the
speeded-up conveyor belt, but not much on who's spreading chemical
fertilizer without protective gear—somebody's there welding tanks two
of my neighbors' sons died in last year—not much reported
on who's making our socks, our ties, our transparent bras and panties, our
Victoria's Secrets, our military uniforms, our kooky Halloween costumes:
Ronald Reagan's mask, the Wolf Man's rubber claws—someone is
making our false teeth, our false dicks, our imitation nails—someone
is working, piecing together the body in the body bag . . . some people
are there . . .

I read the article reporting something documenting 200,000 Jews Baba
Yar massacre, but it's a language cup
the good-hearted like to sip on and feel
non-anti-Semitic about everything unreported, not tabulating
the one hundred forty thousand more piled up
in the same region alone—one hundred forty thousand to the tune
of eleven hundred nine years, just under fourteen thousand per century,
just under a tenth of the last three years
of bombing in Afghanistan and Iraq—
one hundred forty thousand Baba Yarians stabbed, hung, belongings
confiscated, just under a hundred and fifty a year stomped unconscious,
de-titted, kidnapped, corn-holed, de-toothed, ears set on fire.
It's another Absence Article
from the Absence History—there must be a thriving Absence Commodity
Industry in place of the absent journalists—
I'm going to send my Absence Subscription

to the Absence Journal and the Absence Newspaper, I wish all the
Absence Writers, all the Absence People in general,
a long absence off a short pier . . .

The waitress down the counter at my only diner, Nichol's Diner,
complains to her partner, "That old lady's driving me crazy, she wanted
something different with her egg salad—three times—I took it back—
and *you know* what it does to your fingers everyday filling pepper mills—
nobody figures that in."
Some people are there . . .

While I eat my soup they're smoking as they bomb all-night-all-day,
then another takes a dump or jerks off and eats malted protein balls
getting ready to bomb while others bomb and smoke—you can smoke up
there—what, you're going to bomb twenty-four hours a day and have
smoking restrictions? I don't think so.

But I thought
after London-Dresden-Hiroshima-Nagasaki-Tokyo blazes—

I did think
after Mexico City, Kabul, Kent State, Tiananmen Square assassinations—

after the intended invisibilization of Armenians, Gypsies, Afro-everyone

after the bulldozing of Palestinians,
after three million Vietnamese dead, there,
and a million Cambodians dead, there—

I did think
after supporting the six-time succession of Gestapo Twins in the coup of
Chile, the invasion of Guatemala, the Salvadoran civil war,

that the rulers of everything might begin to spare us the serial killing side
of themselves, man I was wrong—a woman's hands on the stairs

with the vein roots from each wrist touching the rail, the cinders, the bone
chips of a boy's shattered something, somebody's arms, what looks like
arms—at the end of the landing,
a womb and the belly-button portion of the skin splotched on the hood
of a truck—

twenty-four hours a day of bombing, *Open All Night*,

the New Flat Earth Society,

Democratika Pathologika—

and you starve in rage over that bloody soup.

Poems from this book previously appeared in the following magazines:

abalonemoon.com: "Bukowski in Love," "Crawdaddy," "Don't Feed the
Sign," "I Went Through a Box of Emily's Shell Jewelry" (as "I Went
Through a Box of Her Jewelry"), "My Hat Up North"
The American Poetry Review: "Howard Mueller's Father" (as "Mueller and
Mueller's Father")
Caliban: "Before and After Tampico"
Cimarron Review: "That Other Aunt"
Exquisite Corpse: "Some Traveling Music"
Iowa Journal of Cultural Studies: "Against Angels"
Kalevala: "Crawdaddy"
Onthebus: "As Much as You Can" (as "The Complaining Root")
Paterson Literary Review: "Four Family"
pemmicanpress.com: "At the Door with Debussy," "Goldwater Died Last
Week," "Latina Worker," "My Piece of the Puzzle," "Natural History,"
"With the Little Esther Phillips of Marseilles"
Poetry International: "The Eighties"
poetrymagazine.com: "Four Family," "What Returns"
Silverfish: "Another Side of Pisgah," "The Kings of Alsea"
10,000poemsproject.com (Hartnell College): "Dvayda," "My Hat Up
North"

Some of the poems in this collection were also published in the chapbooks
Dignity in Naples and North Hollywood, with an introduction by Philip
Levine (Santa Fe: Pennywhistle Press, 1996), and *Onionman* (Los Angeles:
Rabble-A Press, 1999).

In addition:

"Before and After Tampico" appeared in *Homage to Vallejo,* ed.
Christopher Buckley (Santa Cruz, CA: Greenhouse Review Press, 2006)

"Natural History" appeared in *Poets Against the War,* ed. Sam Hamill (New York: Thunder's Mouth Press/Nation Books, 2003), and in *Oakland Out Loud* (Oakland: PEN Press, 2007)

"Predators' Hour 2, Open All Night" appeared on a poster sold to benefit *poetsagainstthewar.org.* The poster was printed by Rabble-A Press (2006) and published online at *pemmicanpress.com.*

Photograph by Linda Janakos

In addition to several chapbooks, Doren Robbins has published five previous full-length collections of poetry, including *Parking Lot Mood Swing: Autobiographical Monologues and Prose Poetry* (Cedar Hills Books, 2004) and *Driving Face Down* (Eastern Washington University Press, 2001), which won the Blue Lynx Prize for Poetry. His poems, prose poems, and short fiction have appeared in a wide array of literary magazines and anthologies, among them the *American Poetry Review, Kayak, Sulphur,* and *For Rexroth,* and have earned him numerous prizes and awards, including a fellowship from Oregon Literary Arts. The cofounder and coeditor of the literary journal *Third Rail,* Robbins has also written critical essays on the work of Charles Bukowski, Deborah Eisenberg, Katerina Gogou, Philip Levine, Larry Levis, Michael McClure, Thomas McGrath, Kenneth Rexroth, Kazuko Shiraishi, Carol Tinker, and Philip Whalen.

Before embarking on a career in teaching, Robbins spent over two decades working as a cook and as a carpenter. His interests extend to art, and he has produced poster-poems to benefit the Salvadoran Medical Relief Fund, *poetsagainstthewar.org,* and PEN. He holds an MFA from the University of Iowa and currently teaches literature and creative writing at Foothill College, in Los Altos, California, where he is director of the Foothill College Writers' Conference.